SAINTS OF ISLAM

HUSAIN R. SAYANI

Qadeem Press

Qadeem Press

Qadeem Press Edition
Breathing Life into Forgotten Pages
www.qadeempress.com

Originally Published by Luzac & Co. in 1908
Reprinted by Qadeem Press in 2025

Find our titles on your favourite online bookstore using the keyword 'Qadeem Press'

Saints of Islam.

PREFACE.

The following pages are intended to give briefly sóme of the main features of the re ligious philosophy of Islam along with a brief account of some of the interesting events of the lives of three of its great Saints. A few of the sentiments ascribed to these saints have been rendered freely into English in order to bring out the spirit of the thought clearly which a literal rendering too often is hardly able to convey, and these thoughts have been compared to similar sentiments of other eminent Oriental thinkers. I have selected the three lives from three different periods in order to survey briefly the development of sōme of the political events and to a small extent the literary advancement effected by the Mohammedans in the course of these periods.

As the interesting events of the lives of great persons great in their moral character and greatness of mind, whether they be of the Christian faith or of any other, are generally found to be interesting and instructive, as such lives contain those strange realities of human life which appeal to the human mind and are instructive to the understanding of human nature; and as there has been of late a keen and growing interest in the literature of the East among the Christian public I have ventured to lay before them the lives of these Muslim saints. Perhaps the title of this book would suggest to some minds the narration of miraculous deeds, of mighty dragons blown out of life by the mere blow of a breath and wild beasts charmed into obedience by simple words of command; or it might suggest perhaps the discussion of subtle metaphysical questions and a vain endeavour to solve the dark mysteries of human life; but instead of finding these if the reader finds in these lives some lessons of true philosophy; if he realizes the truth of these lines —

"What is life worth without a heart to feel
The Great and lovely and the poetry and
Sacredness of things" —

the object of writing this little book would be considered as achieved.

H. R. S.
Bombay,
India.

Saints of Islam.

CHAPTER I.

KHWAJA HASAN AND HIS TIME.

Hasan the handsome was so named because when he was a few days old his mother took him to the Khalif Omar who exclaimed on seeing him "how handsome the child is, name him Hasan" (i. e. handsome). When he grew old he became a jeweller and travelled from one country to another showing his jewels to the Amirs and Nobles of his time. During one of these travels, it is said, he visited Constantinople and had dealings with the Grand Minister. Once the Minister took him out with him telling him "I shall show you to-day a strange sight". When they were outside the city he saw a large royal tent set up with silk strings tied to gold pegs and furnished with silk curtains. Presently he saw a body of armed soldiers in their full uniform taking a round of the tent and uttering some words in a low voice. They went away after taking the round and a number of venerable old men with gray beards followed and did the same ceremony over. After them came the chief councillors of the state and lastly some beautiful damsels with gold trays laden with gems and jewels over their heads. They too performed the same ceremony. When all had gone away, the king with his minister entered the tent, and after a while they came out and the king left the place with tears in his eyes. Hasan was greatly surprised and asked the minister what it meant. He said "The Emperor had a son handsome and accomplished, bold in war and wise in council, whom his father loved with all his heart. The prince suddenly fell ill, and in spite of all the efforts made to save his life he succumbed to his illness. This tent is set up over his tomb for the annual ceremony in his memory which is performed in this wise. A body of soldiers in their full uniform and bearing their arms commence the ceremony by taking the round of the tent and uttering these words while so doing "Oh Prince if it lay in our power to avert what befell thee with the strength of our arms, our service was ready for thee. But strength and arms avail not against Him by whom thy fate was decreed". Then follow venerable old men uttering the words while taking their round "Our intercession was ready for thee but intercession avails not with one whose decrees are final". Then the councillors of the State repeating "if our craft and cunning could have averted thy death we would surely have exerted them in thy favour. But craft is in vain against the All-Knowing Providence". Lastly the beautiful damsels uttering the words "Our charms were ready to do thee service "Oh Prince" but this was from Him who is not affected in any way by beauty's wiles and beauty's tears". The king then enters the tent with his minister and says "Oh Prince I would have sold my whole kingdom to save thy life but kings are as helpless against death as the poorest of their subjects". It is said that this scene weighed so heavily on Hasan's mind that henceforth all his endeavours were to prepare himself against Death. He settled at Bussora and led a pious life and spent his time in the service of his fellow creatures.

Perhaps no theme is oftener dwelt upon by Oriental Authors than Death. Its grim side as well as its bright side, for even grim Death has its bright side, are depicted in the peculiar vein of Oriental style. They delight to depict Death as the unconquerable conqueror that snatches away the crown from the powerful monarch's head and lowers him from his throne to the bier; the all-levelling leveller that puts the meanest slave on an equal footing with his master and the poorest subject with his powerful sovereign; the ever present Instructor teaching us the lesson that worldly glory and the vain pursuits of this life end in nothingness; It is also a consoler consoling the afflicted and the wronged one that their miseries will soon come to an end, and comforting the bereaved one that he has only to pass Death's bridge to enter the land where he will have no more to suffer the pangs of separation.

Every scene of life has its humorous side and Sadi in one of his odes describes the humorous side of Death and we have tried to give below the humour of the sentiment expressed in that ode. The picture needless to say is drawn from the Oriental way of life. —

How sad the hour when Life's concluding game
Waits the last move of Checkmate and of Death
When the weak frame wearied with its life-long work
Lies on the bed, to seek its last repose in Death.
How sad to see the few last efforts of the loving friends
To save a life whose cup of time is filled
For what avails all care and cleverness
'Gainst Nature's final laws or Fate's decree.
Still in that hour hope clings to the dying man
When Med'-cine fails, the aid of amulets, and incantations sought,
Concluding still 'tis the *Hakim's* fault
For matters would not come to such a pass the otherwise
While Life's frail ship lies rolling, its sails all lost,
How sad to think what passes over the troubled mind
Perhaps the thought of evil done in this short life
Its swift gliding realized
The dread of evil end, for evil done to others
For the passing good of transient Life, whose end is seen so near
At last the sad news given out, how sad the scene
The house it rings with *Mulla's* prayers
Swift and loud for paid with ready coin
The first rites o'er the priests have still their time, engaged
In vain ceremonies, kept for some months, at regular intervals
For custom hath decreed it more than love;
Pure faith based on love is simplest in its form
Free of cumbrous ceremonies and various rites
The device of cunning priests, to gain a living in a fellow creature's death.
Sweetmeats and fruits given to fill the fakir's mouth
Fat and pampered,

Perhaps more worthy to be kept on fasts than fed with sweets
Thus fed that they may bless the dead man's soul
Sincerely if sincerity be purchased.
Then comes another scene,
The wrangles betwixt the beneficiaries
Trying each to rob the other of his right
The house, the shop, the garden, all appraised,
Perchance the *Cazi* has the lion's share
For power has this attribute
Of drawing money to itself
By crooked means in mismanaged states.
Last scene of all, Love's last act
The dear spouse that wets her eyes with tears
Love's flow which hath its ebb like other things
Forgetting soon the past
She weds another — the scene here ends at last.

Before however proceeding further with Hasan's account we should take a brief survey of the time in which he lived (19 A.H to 110 A.H.). Hasan was born at Medina in the year 19 A.H. and died 110 A.H. living to the ripe old age of 91. He had seen the fourth Khalif, Ali, when that personage came to Bussora and visited the chief mosques of that city giving orders that none should ascend the pulpit and preach to the faithful except those who had proved themselves worthy of that office. Perhaps the greatest harm done to religion and to society in general is by its illiterate and narrow-minded priests who preach only to gain notoriety or make a living out of it. But Ali found in Hasan a true and worthy preacher and he was allowed to preach.

In the natural course of events that followed after the holy Prophet's death, the purity of religious sentiment and the enthusiasm for truth that had governed the minds of those who were Islam's first votaries, and which had contributed in a great degree to bring about the establishment of a growing Mohamedan Empire, had already begun to be alloyed by selfish motives and a desire of mere temporal power. It came to a culminating point when on one side Imam Husain the noble grandson of the Prophet stood for the purity of religion and on the other side Yazid moved simply by a desire to gain temporal power and the enjoyment of worldly pleasures opposed him. The field of Karbala had decided for Yazid. The first four Khalifs had lived in the simplest possible style. All the state-revenue in their time had been spent for state purposes. In Yazid's time appeared the first signs of that luxury and royal state for which subsequently the Mohamedan kings became distinguished among monarchs of other nations. Islam had laid down the principle that the Ruler of the Faithful should be the Defender of his Faith too. It required in the sovereign a moral character above reproach, and an unalloyed intention to serve the people for the Love of the Lord and not for any selfish motive. The Prophet had said "the leader of a people is their servant and should serve them". The struggle for preserving this principle in practice continued, though weakly, after Husain. Abdulla bin Zaid one of the citizens of Mecca had raised the standard of revolt against Yazid's descendant Merwan bin Abdul Malik who was the Khalif of that time. The Khalif after delivering the Friday sermon in the Jam-e-Musjid of Kufa asked any one of the congregation to come forward and lead an army against the Meccans. But as yet the love of the people was so much for the purity of religion and for the sacred city of the Prophet's birth-place that no one would come forward, and lead an army for this purpose; when Hajjaj a young man of exceptional abilities but without any scruples of conscience came forward and undertook to do the job for the Khalif. By degrees, this man rose to power till he became the Governor of Irak during Hasan's life time.

Hajjaj the tyrant.

This Hajjaj is the Nero of Mahomedan history. Some of the historical works written by Persian authors contain some interesting pages regarding the history of this man. Although of a very tyrranical nature he was not without a ghastly humour of his own as is shown by the following stories related of him. It is said he delighted in spilling human blood. Once when out hunting with his Amirs, in the hot pursuit of a chase his horse led him far away from his attendants into a sandy plain, and the trying heat of the tropical sun and the fatigue of the chase made him very thirsty. He looked in vain for a long time for some human habitation. At last after wandering a good deal he espied a cottage and found an old woman therein. He told her to appease his thirst which was killing him and the old woman brought him a cup of water. He told her that in recompense for saving his life he would reward her if she came any day to his court. The old woman was delighted with the expectation of a great reward and went a few days later to his court. Hajjaj said "Look here old woman thou didst appease my thirst and saved my life that was flowing out of me, by a sweet cup of water. What better recompense can I give thee than giving thee to drink the sweet cup of martyrdom than which there is no sweeter cup to the faithful and which gives him eternal life in paradise, a rare gift for which the faithful must ever be thankful". All the protestations of the poor woman were in vain against his tyrranical nature and she had to drink the sweet cup of martyrdom and forfeit her life for her misplaced act of charity.

Another time while riding out of the town he found a rustic sitting alone and his sense of humour being aroused he went near the rustic and said "Dost thou know Hajjaj the governor of these provinces? What sort of a fellow is he"? The rustic replied "He is a blood-thirsty tyrant". "And dost thou know me" Hajjaj said," I am Hajjaj the son of Yusuf the ruler of these provinces". The rustic had a ready mind and he answered "Dost thou know me? I am the son of an Amir and I suffer from a malady which turns me mad three days every month and to-day is one of those days". Hajjaj could not but admire the fellow's cheek and humour.

It is said a pious man who was reputed amongst the Muslims as one whose prayers always hit the mark of acceptance in the Divine Court visited Bussora and Hajjaj was informed of his arrival. He sent for him and told him to pray for him his best prayer. The pious man raised his hands in prayer and said "Oh Lord take away this tyrant's life". Hajjaj exclaimed "for God's sake what are you about". "My prayer" he replied "would free thee from thy evil nature and the muslims from thy tyranny". It however took some time for the acceptance of the Derwish's prayers in the Court of God, and Hajjaj lived for some years more to tyrranize over the people.

In his last moments too the tyrant was not

without his ghastly humour. He asked his astrologer who was near his death-bed whether he (the astrologer) had found in his astrological calculations that a ruler of note would die in those days. He replied he had found out from his calculations that a ruler of the name of Kulaib would die in the near future. "Of a truth" said the tyrant, "My name is Kulaib (doggie) although no one knows it for my mother used to call me by that name. But I would make thee a fore-runner for me for I might have recourse to the services of a cunning fellow like thee in the regions where I go", and the astrologer found to his cost that some words are better left unsaid.

It is worth noticing that when Hajjaj was Governor of Irak he prepared an expedition from Bussora the chief city of Irak, under the Khalif's order for the invasion of India and gave its command to his nephew Abul Kasim. Of the subsequent history of the expedition we need not write as every reader of Indian history is familiar with it. But there is a halo of romance around Abul Kasim's tragic fate. He had sent two beautiful Indian

Princesses taken as prisoners of war for the Khalif's harem. One of them with the idea of wreaking vengence on the chief whose sword had laid to dust her father's kingdom told the Khalif who was captivated with her charming beauty that she was unworthy of his bed for Abul Kasim had defiled her before he sent her to the Khalif. The Khalif's wrath was kindled and he sent a peremptory order to Abul Kasim to get himself sewed up in a sack and order his men to bring the sack to the Khalif. Abul Kasim it is said, faithful to his master's order did what he was bid to do though he had to pay it with his life. It is said the Khalif subsequently found out Abul Kasim's innocence and put the wily princess to death. The story if true, shows at any rate, the faithfulness of the general, a national characteristic for which Mahomedans are distinguished amongst other Oriental nations.

Hasan generally preached on Friday the Sabbath day of the Mahomedans before a large congregation. He was bold in his speech and never feared to speak out the truth though he had sometimes to risk his personal safety for it. One of our sages says that God appoints a Pharoah for him whom he loveth, to try his patience and the saint had his Pharoah in the tyrant Governor. Once while the saint was preaching on the blessings of having a good and just ruler and was depicting the character of a tyrant in bold colours the Governor entered the Musjid with his soldiers, with drawn swords and took his seat amonst the congregation. The people said to one another "Now will Hasan bridle his tongue for the safety of his dear life"; but Hasan went on boldly with his theme growing warmer and warmer over it till Hajjaj even admired his boldness and rose and said "If anyone would like to see a bold fellow, here is one in the person of Hasan". But though the tyrant appreciated the Saint's true worth, he was a slave to his tyrranic nature as every tyrant is, and the saint had to suffer many a persecution from his hands. The saint's sufferings, however came to an end by the tyrant's death and he had the consolation to see the people freed from the tyrant's *zulum*.

It is remarkable with what a peculiar sort

of pleasure and a smile of gratitude we look back upon our sufferings suffered for a true cause whether that cause may have triumphed or not. Life's path though strewn with thorns, when traversed, with virtue and righteousness as one's guides and a noble object in one's view looks after all, a fair one when we look back upon it and the sentiment is well expressed in the lines of the Persian Poet Jalal when he says.

"The country which I traversed looked to me a fair one after all, when I looked back upon it. Though the dust of mishaps was all along my path it was perhaps purposely laid there that I should clean it off from my garments with my tears. If I tripped and fell away for a time from Thee it was even so for Thy will decreed it to teach me something. If I was not allowed to be near Thee unless I passed the kennels of Thy dogs who barked and snapped at me, the thought that Thou wast near and that I would soon reach Thee was consolation enough for me and after all to be united with Thee atoned for all the pain and sufferings I suffered in Thy Love".

Ibn Sirrin the Interpreter of Dreams.

Another notable figure in Hasan's time was Ibne Sirrin who figures in Mohamedan history as the true interpreter of dreams. It is said that in interpreting dreams he would note the hour when it was dreamt, the season of the year, the peculiar natural aspect at the time and the physical and mental condition of the dreamer. Many interesting stories are told of the way in which he interpreted dreams. A person came to him and said that he had dreamt that night that some one gave him seventy leaves of a tree. The interpreter told him that he would receive seventy thousand dirhams (a small silver coin) in a few days. It so happened that a few days later, the person obtained a service under Government and getting into the good graces of the Khalif for a distinguished act of service which pleased the Khalif he obtained from him the seventy thousand dirhams fore-told by the interpreter. A few months later another person had the same dream and he came before the interpreter for its interpretation. He told him he would receive seventy lashes of the switch in a few days, and it happened as he had fore-told. The people were surprised and asked the interpreter the reason of the contrary turning out of the same dream. He replied "when the former person came to me the leaves were green on the trees and the branches were thick with fruit. While when the latter came the season had changed and the trees had only dry branches of which switches are made".

According to the belief of the Muslims, prophets and saints have true dreams for there being no mist of sins to cloud their vision, their pure spirit sees the coming event on the horizon of time before it actually happens, which the ordinary eye cannot descry. Next to the prophets and saints, according to them, as regards dreaming true dreams, come the righteous king, solicitous about the welfare of his subjects, the old man nearing his death and the faithful and loving wife always true to the interests of her husband.

Ibn Sirrin interpreted aright about Hasan's death. One of his friends told him that he had seen in his dream that night that a bird suddenly dropped down from the heavens and picking up the fairest pebble from the Musjid's compound flew away with it. "If thou speakest truth" he said, "Hasan will soon be picked away from us by death for he is the most pious man amongst us," and so it happened.

Hasan was so humble that he never thought himself better than any of his fellow creatures. One day passing by the banks of the Tigris he saw a negro on the spree, with a woman in his company, and a bottle of wine placed before him. Hasan said to himself "Perhaps I am better than he, for I am no drunkard neither am I immoral with women". As he was engaged in this train of thought a boat passed along the waters and caught by a sudden blast of wind it capsized. The crew seven in number struggled in the water for their lives. The negro jumped in and saved one after another six of the number and turning to Hasan said "Come along save the seventh for thou thinkest thyself better than me. I am no drunkard. The bottle contains only water and the woman is my mother". Hasan never afterwards considered himself better than any of his fellow creatures.

A story is told about the Saint's love of the lower animals. He bargained to purchase a horse of one of his acquaintances, for the dumb creature had got maimed and had excited the Saint's pity. The acquaintance was only too glad to get rid of it. Next day the acquaintance saw in his dream a fair plot of land in heaven and a beautiful horse grazing on it and inquiring to whom it belonged, he was told that it belonged to Hasan the lover of lower animals. Next day the Saint's acquaintance went before him and asked of him as a favour to cancel the bargain as he said from what he had seen in his dream the previous night, he now appreciated how noble it was to be kind to the dumb creatures. But the Saint would not cancel the bargain, for the Saint had seen the same dream that night, and the acquaintance left his house disappointed. Next night the Saint saw in his dream a spacious mansion in Heaven far better than the plot of land and the horse grazing upon it which he had seen the previous night, and inquiring to whom it belonged he was told that it belonged to the person who was lenient in his dealings with his fellow creatures and treated them with love and kindness. The Saint next day went to his acquaintance, and according to the desire of the acquaintance cancelled the bargain.

That Hasan appreciated the responsibility of a leader can be gathered from his taking a lesson to his heart from an answer he received from a drunkard, whom he saw reeling and going on with unsteady steps in one of the muddy streets of Bussora. He told him to keep his steps steady otherwise he might get a bad fall, whereupon the drunkard answered "Oh Iman of the Muslims I would clean myself of the dirt easily enough if I tripped, but it would be sad both for thee and thy followers if thou trippest, and couldst scarce clean thyself of the dirt that would cling to thee for ages". Hasan took the lesson to heart and told his followers to warn him instantly they found him in the wrong.

Hasan had a keen sense of humour and even trifles would give him food for reflexion.

Seeing a child carrying a candle he asked him whence had the light of the candle come. The child remained embarrased for a time but presently a blast of wind blew out the light and the child said in triumph "Tell me Sir where has it disappeared and I shall tell you whence did it come" Thus Life's flickering flame appears from whence one scarcely knows, and vanishes by a sudden blast of death. The sentiment is well expressed in the lines of the poet Rumi where speaking of Life and Death he says—

"It was a speck of colour that appearing on the horizon of human life from the one colourless ocean of Divinity, remained there for a while, and losing again its colour of individuality it vanished into the colourless sphere from whence it had come".

Hasan says "a woman's answer once went right to my soul. She came running to me with bare hands and head complaining of her husband's conduct towards her. I asked her to go and cover herself properly and then come to me. She said 'Imam of the Muslims I have so lost my senses in the love of a creature that I am not conscious of my own self. Hadst thou not informed me of it, I would have run on to the Bazar unconscious of my not being properly covered; but wert thou as much in love with thy Creator as I am with one of His creatures thou wouldst not have looked to my bare arms and head'.

Hasan says "I was on the terrace of my house when I heard my neighbour's wife giving the following warm sermon to her husband. She began — 'Hast thou lost thy sense; I have been with thee for these forty years, thy partner in all thy sufferings. I never complained of thee even if thou didst not supply me with my wants and endured for thee the cold of winter and the hot weather of summer. I kept thy respect in thy fellow creatures' eyes and submitted to thy slightest wish. But I will never never submit to this thing. Thou wantest to take another partner in thy love prefering her to me. I will never allow thine eyes to settle on another woman's beauty. I will seize the Imam's skirt and complain bitterly of thee before him". Hasan says this reminded him of the Lord's words,

"Verily God forgiveth not the taking of other partners unto Him but other than this he forgiveth to whom He pleaseth". The love that one should bear towards his Lord must be unalloyed, pure and selfless.

We give below some of Hasan's words comparing the sentiment with the similar sentiments expressed by other Mahomedan thinkers of note —

To one who asked what is Patience Patience is two-folded, its one-fold lies in suffering affliction with a cheerful mind resigning oneself to the Will of the Lord; the other in restraining oneself from indulgence in things forbidden by the Lord.

The man having praised Hasan's patience and piety he replied — Nay, *that* piety is best which is born of the love one bears to his Lord whilst it may be that mine be out of a desire to get the good things of Heaven; and *that* patience is best which proceeds out of love to conform to the Divine pleasure, dreading to fall away from Him — while it may be that mine be due only to a dread of the torture of Hell; for true love should allow no alloy of simply centering one's hopes on any created thing forgetting the creator or of doing anything which love requires to be done, simply out of a dread of some thing which we don't like to suffer". Sadi has a similar sentiment where he says "Oh nightingale thou warblest in vain; take to thy heart the instance of the moth; it burns itself in love of the lamp light without uttering any noise; for the lovers, their self extinguished, live only in their loved one's love and no utterance of complaint comes from one who is dead to himself.

2. The true standard of judging the worth of a person's knowledge lies in its beneficial effect upon its possessor; of deed in its being effective, of love in its being sincere, of contentment in its independence of things earthly, and of patience in its being due to a sincere love of the Lord. Whoever is truly possessed of these, I would not be surprised if his Lord poureth on him all His blessings.

3. A sheep is better than an un-awakened human being, for the sheep is called away by the shepherd's voice from grazing on

weeds that would harm him; but the word of God does not call away a human being steeped in pleasures of this world from self-indulgence.

4. There is no greater pestilence on this earth than one who always utters vain words; and whosoever remains silent without observing and judging upon things around him is deeply set in ignorance; and the glance which goes without drawing a lesson goes in vain.

5. Whosoever is sound in sense has always moments of silent contemplation and communion with his heart, searching out and discovering in those moments truths which lay hidden before and which leap up on his tongue when the occasion calls them forth.

6. It is no slander to expose three persons, the person who always indulges his passions, the adulterer and the oppressive ruler who practises *zulum* over his subjects. Compare the Koran "God loveth not that evil be matter of public talk unless any one hath been wronged and God is the Hearing, the Knowing."

7. The best reins are those that thou puttest on thy refractory self.

8. Sincere piety reaches the point where nothing but truth comes upon the tongue of its possessor whether he be in temper or out of temper; where his limbs are never used amiss in the perpetration of that which is forbidden by the Lord, where not a single thought passes his mind which is not approved of His Lord. Compare the similar sentiment in Jami where he says —

"Nothing can extinguish true love's fire for it is the spiritual in man which ignites it. The ring dove can as soon remove the natural ring around its neck as the lover remove the fetters of obedience put round his neck by Love's hands".

9. If I knew myself quite free from hypocracy I would love myself more than any other creature on the face of this Earth.

Saints of Islam.

CHAPTER II.

IBN ADHAM OR THE SAINT-KING.

SULTAN IBRAHIM OF BALKH SON OF SULAIMAN ADHAM BIN MANSUR.

"Whosoever loveth and is chaste in his love, and hideth it, and dieth in it dieth a Martyr" (Hadis or saying of the prophet).

Ibn Adham's father was a prince but his heart was given to piety. He left his country and became a derwish. A derwish, according to his creed, must pass his life in such a way as to gain ultimately that purity in which he should see the reflection of the Supreme Beauty of his Creator; consequently he passes his time in good deeds, in prayers and the contemplation of Divine attributes, and of His Beauty reflected in Nature. The holy Koran repeatedly appeals to the mind of the reader, to read Nature's Book and to reflect on its contents; for instance in the Sura, where the Lord sayeth — "Verily in the creation of the Heavens and of the Earth; and in the alternation of night and day and the ship which glideth upon the sea with what is useful to man, and in what the Lord sendeth down of the rain from Heaven reviving thereby the Earth after its death; and in the scattering over the Earth of all the moving creatures, and in the sending of winds and the clouds that move between the Heaven and the Earth, are signs unto those that exercise their reason". And in the saying of the prophet "An hour's contemplation is better than a year's prayers".

The derwish travelled by day and passed his nights in prayers and contemplation. At last he came to Balkh, at that time a famous and populous city in the Oriental world, and passing through its streets paused at the palace of the king, probably thinking of his own palace and the good things he had left behind. The Princess seeing the derwish came to the window to bestow a coin upon him. The poor derwish was smitten in love with her beauty. Her charming beauty had ensnared him. He might well describe himself in some such sentiments as the oriental poets delight to indulge in — "Those charms of the watery tulips of thy lips and the languishing narcissuses of thy eyes — sometime redden my face like the tulip with the thought of thy union — sometimes droop me down like the narcissus with the dread of thy separation". The derwish would not move from his place. Day after day he was there to catch one more glimpse of the charming beauty of the Princess. The king was in wrath and would have put him to death, but justice required otherwise. The king ordered him to come into his presence. He saw that the derwish was of no ordinary kind and was struck with his refined manners and daring conduct. "What wouldst thou have of me" he said. "Thy daughter's hand", the derwish replied. "Her *mahar* is two precious gems of the size of a bird's egg", the king said. The derwish left the Court. It is related he went to the sea-shore and engaged himself in prayers and devotions asking Divine aid to help him. His prayers were accepted and Khizar appeared before him. Thrusting his hands into the waves he brought out the desired gems and presented them to the derwish. The derwish next day went to the king and in full court presented the gems to him. The king was non-plussed, and finding the Princess willing to wed the derwish, the engagement was ratified and the day fixed for the wedding. But before the appointed day a report was given out that the Princess was dead. The lover was distracted. One sudden autumn blast of death had withered the spring flower of his hope and scattered it to the winds. He followed the bier to the graveyard, which was outside the city, as was usually the case in those days. When the people departed he lingered in the grave-yard to get a last glimpse at her, if opportunity offered, and to feast his eyes for the last time with her supreme beauty. At dusk when there was no one near about, he took out the body from the mound of earth, but just as he was looking upon her he heard a noise and some robbers appeared upon the scene. He hastily concealed himself. It so happened that there was a person among the robbers who was once a clever *Hakim*, but by some freak of fortune had turned a robber. After gazing at the Princess' face for a while he exclaimed "She is in a stupor on account of some drug administered to her; she is not dead". He took out a drug from his pocket and put it in her mouth. After a while the Princess opened her eyes. The lover could not contain himself. He sprung out from his concealment and made for the robbers. They were taken by surprise and took to their heels. In a short time the Princess recovered her senses completely and the two lovers left the place to settle somewhere far from the city of Balkh; which they did in a quiet cottage, where under such romantic circumstances Ibrahim Ibn Adham, popularly called Bin Adham, was born, about the end of the first century of the Mahomedan Hejira. He grew up in that cottage where Love and piety reigned supreme. His mother died when he was only a boy, and his father thinking to give him a fit education brought him to the city of Balkh and put him to school. The boy went daily to school and one day his grand-mother happening to pass that way, was struck with the boy's extraordinary resemblance in his features, to her dead daughter. Her suspicions were aroused and after a complete inquiry the boy was found out to be her own grand-son and was taken to the family bosom as the Lost Joseph returning once more to Canaan. In the course of time his grandfather died and left the throne to Ibn Adham.

Ibne Adham was now in his full youth, with the absolute powers of an Oriental Potentate, and blest with all the luxuries which human heart could desire. But he had early imbibed his father's piety and his sentiments in the little cottage of his childhood, where not only piety but Love which chasteneth it and gives its sovereign seal to it, which alone makes it acceptable in the Divine Court, had reigned supreme. He knew that mere dry piety was at best a weak disciplinarian, a tutor with but scanty knowledge and without any firmness of character or refinement of sentiment who could scarcely mould the character of his pupils or influence their sentiments. He had begun to realize that he should awaken within himself that inward eye, before whose keen glance the innumerable curtains that have preceded and will follow our present life should rise one by one and reveal to the spectator a considerable portion of Creation's play from its beginning to the end of its one ever lasting scene. In fact his mind was just awakening to the mystery of the human soul which had puzzled many a great mind before him, and which nature reveals to her few chosen ones — when he received signs after signs from his Divine Instructor which worked powerfully on the state of his mind.

It is related that as he was one night engaged in his devotions he heard a voice upon the roof of his room. When he questioned it the voice answered "I am searching my lost camel here". "How canst thou find it on the roof of a king's palace", he said. The voice replied "Oh Ibn Adham canst thou find thy Lord in a king's palace"?

A few days later when he came to his room one evening after his usual devotions, he saw his royal bed occupied by one of his slave girls. Ibn Adham was highly vexed with the girl but she only smiled at him on seeing him angry. His curiosity was aroused and he questioned her about it. She answered "Oh Sire it is only for a few moment's gratification of my vanity to occupy a royal bed that I suffer my master's anger. Wouldst thou not incur thy Master's anger for all thy self-indulgence and the gratification of thy vain desires?"

A few days after this, it is said, he received another sign which went right to his soul. One day as he was on his throne in full state of royalty with the Amirs all around him, each one kissing the humble ground of obeisance before his feet and standing in his place with bowed neck and folded hands ready to obey the slightest sign from his master's eye, an unknown person entered the court and passing boldly through the line of Amirs stood before his throne, and demanded whether he could give him a shelter in his inn. "Is this an inn?" the king exclaimed "this is a king's palace". "And pray Sir who was before you in this palace?" the person asked; "My father"; "and before that?"; "My grandfather and so on" was the reply. "Is this then not an inn" the person said "a sojourning place where the incomer after a short-lived hospitality marches forth on his onward journey?". So saying the person disappeared. Ibn Adham's mind was highly perturbed. He realized he had to make the best of his short sojourn in this world to gain whatever might be of avail on his onward march. He became restless with these thoughts, and he thought to beguile his mind from them by going for a hunt with his Amirs. He gathered his Amirs and set out for that purpose. In the heat of the chase he pursued a deer which led him far away from his Amirs. In the excitement of his mind he heard the deer utter to him "Oh Ibn Adham leave me alone for thou art Love's chase". The lamp of his soul was kindled. He was put in mind of the words of his Lord "when I love him (the righteous man) I become his ears with which he hears, and his eyes with which he sees and his hands with which he handles and his feet with which he walks". Ibn Adham realized that he must acquire Divine ears to hear His words and the secrets of Nature, he must have Divine eyes to see the Supreme beauty of the Creator, and have Divine feeling to feel every pulse and spring with which nature is guided.

Leaving the chase Ibn Adham passed on and when he had gone far from Balkh he alighted from his horse and seeing a peasant working in a field he exchanged his royal dress with him, and gave him his horse. The next several years he spent in self-instruction and in the acquirement of his cherished object. Some part of this time he spent in a cave near a village, only coming out once or twice a week to earn his scanty meal with the sweat of his brow, half of which meal he gave to the needy, retaining the other half for himself.

In after-years he used to desribe the hardships he endured during this period. "Once" he said" "it was so cold that it was frozen all around the cave. I broke pieces of ice and took my bath with them. I yearned for some warm covering, but I had none. Presently I felt myself wrapped up in something warm, and sleep came upon me. I had a quiet nap for some hours. When I awoke I saw to my great surprise that it was a great dragon that had wrapt me up and I prayed 'Oh Lord thou didst send it in the garb of Thy mercy, but I now see it in its own garb which is that of Thy wrath'. The Dragon gently removed itself from me".

THIRD STAGE.

The second stage in this Saint's Life was now complete. He had now thrown off the dross of "Self" and retained the pure gold of selfless love. He was now the Sikander of his time, for he had built a solid wall between his pure self and the gog and the magog of evil passions, and selfish desires. No syren voice of "self" can now allure his spirit down. We might now echo the sentiment of the poet "Sanai" regarding him —

"It takes days, before the wool on a sheep's back be turned into a derwish's garb or a cord for the ass's neck; weeks, before the cotton seed sown in the moist ground produce the stuff, which by the aid of human art be turned into a bride's apparel, or a martyr's pall; months, before the sperm turns into an infant — a future hero to lead victorious legions to break the enemies ranks; years, before the stone turns into a priceless jewel; generations, before a true poet be born to delight mankind with his exquisite poetry, or a philosopher to change the sentiments of mankind; but it takes *centuries*, before a *true man of God* be born who seeing his Lord with his inward eye, lead erring, blind humanity to the path of virtue, of righteousness, of Love".

We shall now give some instances related of our Saint's endurance for the love of Him for Whom he had forsaken his earthly kingdom, his love of human kind, his charitable mind in the truest sense of the word and last but not least the good he did for human kind. In relating these instances we should not forget that he was once a powerful potentate blest with all the luxuries that human heart could desire. The contrast must have been keen. The poor peasant endures the hustles of the world with patience because he is inured to it from his childhood, and after a time does not see anything out of the way in it. The needy is humble because it is his interest to be so. But it must have been different with one who was once a powerful king. He endured it all with a good humour, which never failed him, and a sweetness of temper never soured by any hardship. Once while on a ferry boat he had with him a set of rowdy Amirs who finding him a derwish made him the butt of their raillery and played all sorts of practical jokes upon him. His endurance was put to a sore trial, but he did not lose his composure. He must have been vividly reminded of the time when the Amirs kissed the ground of obeisance before his feet, and stood with bent necks to obey his slightest order; who crouched with fear to see their king angry, and were thirsty to gain his slightest approbation. At last Divine inspiration came unto his pure heart and whispered "if thou desirest they shall be meted out with grievous punishment"; But his humble prayer was "O Lord I remember thy Hundred Names each bespeaking the peculiar phase of thy Mercy except one 'Al-Kahhar' (the Avenger) which speakst of thine anger. Give them the eyes to see between right and wrong". His prayer was accepted and they saw before them one crowned with the Light of Divine Glory, with a Halo of Divine Light all around him. They fell at his feet and asked for mercy.

Once wrapt up in his own thoughts he sat on a Musjid's front steps. Presently the *Muezzin* came and pushed him so roughly that he fell some steps below. He said in after years regarding this incident that he only wished the Musjid had more steps, for every fall from the steps gave him an inward vision such as he would not sell for the kingdom of both the worlds.

Such and similar treatment he received while he was unknown; but such a character and intellect as his was, could not long be hidden. He travelled much and his fame in spite of his unwillingness grew apace. Where-ever he went his words of wisdom and the purity of his character worked upon the sentiments of the people.

In those days when the means of communication were scanty, when no state aid was given to clergymen to live in all the comforts, nay luxury of life, and to keep the public conscience straight; when there were no great public funds for the Salvationists to go forth to foreign lands to beat the tomtoms and make a grand *tamasha*, in those days a more solid work was done for blind humanity by the voluntary efforts of persons who, possessing a purity of life and a greatness and nobleness of mind such as is rarely found in our present age, have left foot-prints on the path of human life to guide for ever the erring to the path of selfless love and righteousness.

The last years of Ibn Adham's life and activities were spent at the Holy Musjid of Mecca. He lived during the reign of three successive Khalifs of Bagdad, Harun-Ar-Rashid, Mamun and Mutasim-Billah, the last of whom is said to have visited him and conferred with him. The influence of a great Murshid or a true saint in a Mahomedan kingdom is such as can scarcely be conceived by those who do not belong to that creed. In his holy *Darbar* worldly distinctions are done away with. The poorest peasant may take his seat beside the proudest monarch. Rulers and chiefs kiss the hands of the holy man with reverance and join their hands with his in solemn *baiat* (or a pledge with their lives to be guided by him). He is often the Mediator between the king and his subjects in redressing their wrongs and obtaining justice from the powerful monarch's hands, and such influence he exercises not by any temporal power placed in his hands, for he never cares to have any, but by the moral force of his character and the greatness of his mind.

In the *mausam* (or period) of Hajj or the sacred pilgrimage when a stream of pilgrims from every part of the world gathered in that holy city, Ibn Adham's pure words like Israfeel's trumpet must have enlivened many a spirit dead with wrong-doing in its body-grave. Like many other sacred relics the pilgrims must have carried with them his words and the various remembrances of his pure life to all the parts of the world.

A large circle of disciples gathered round the saint. The first condition that he made with the person who desired to enter his circle was that he should eat only of what was lawfully gained. He himself went daily to the forest to cut wood, and in exchange for it had loaves of bread and dates which he distributed among his disciples, retaining only a scanty portion of it for himself. Many instances are related of his love of mankind and his truly charitable mind. While staying with some fellow-derwishes in the midst of winter in an old creaking Musjid, which had a door full of holes like a sieve, he stood for the whole night before the door to keep the bitter from wind beating against his poor friends

While travelling with a fellow-derwish his friend fell ill. The Saint nursed him most tenderly and spent all he had with him. As his friend wanted some more comforts the Saint sold his riding donkey and procured them for him. When his friend became well they set out again on their travel; but as his friend did not like the idea of walking all along as he felt still a little weak, the Saint carried him full three *manzals* on his back.

While passing through a street he saw a man dead-drunk, his face and mouth filthy with the drink. The saint fetched water and cleansed his face and mouth with it saying "it is not meet that the mouth which uttereth God's name should remain filthy". When the man heard of what the saint had done, he repented of his folly and cured himself of his bad habit.

The saint's good humour never failed him. While going to the forest to cut wood a proud *lashkari* (common soldier) mistook him for a slave and accosting him roughly asked the way to the *abadani* (an inhabited place). The saint replied "I am no doubt a bondsman", and pointed to the grave-yard meaning *there* is the population. This vexed the proud soldier and he assaulted the saint. The people gathered and when the fellow knew whom he had assaulted, he fell on his knees and asked for mercy. The saint replied "I blest thee for it for the wronged one is nearer his Lord than the wrong doer. I answered thee aright for I am His bondsman, and the grave-yard daily gets an increase in its population while the city now-a-days is getting depopulated".

When asked whether he had ever seen a truly charitable person the saint replied "At

Mecca I went to an hair-dresser and having nothing with me to pay him I said 'Trim my hairs for thy Lord's sake'. He kissed my forehead and trimmed my hairs as he would have trimmed a king's or an Amir's. I told him I would pay him whatever I get at the very first opportunity. A little while after this, one of my disciples sent me a purse of pure gold dinars. I took the purse to the hair-dresser and offered it to him. He said 'Oh Ibn Adham what a simpleton thou art. Didst thou not say "Do it for thy Lord's sake." I did it for His love and I wont't have anything in return for it'. I said 'Look here, these are Dinars of pure gold'. He answered 'Oh miser! true wealth lies in the possession of a rich mind and not in gold and silver.' "

If a derwish share his scanty meal, honestly gained by the sweat of his brow, with his brother derwish, it is perhaps an act of charity more acceptable in the sight of God than the giving away of some superfluous thousands by a millionaire, which did not add to his comforts but which were rather an encumbrance unto him and which he generally gives for gaining vain titles and earthly glory. We do not for a moment deny the fact that these thousands contribute to the comforts of his fellow brothers, and relieve their sufferings. But the question is whether such charity goes to enrich the heart of the donor; the spirit can only redeem itself by paying the ransom of Divine selfless Love. The smallest coin of action with the stamp of Love upon it, and unalloyed by a selfish motive, contributes to this ransom. "If thou beamest upon thy fellow-brother with a smile it is charity." "If thou fillest his bucket with water from thy own it is charity". It is always humble because it looks to the greatness and goodness of God. The Persian Poet perhaps felt the same emotion when he spoke in exaggerated terms in the manner of his own kind" "If there be an ant endowed with speech; if there be an hair endowed with life and love, I am *that* ant and I am *that* hair".

That our saint knew how noble is the pain of love can be gathered from his answer to a day-labourer, who, returning home one evening dejected and sorrowful, for he had not earned his wages for the day to supply his family with the evening meal, saw the Saint sitting in all composure and envied him his lot. The saint replied "I would gladly exchange all my righteous deeds for this thy hour's selfless sorrow for those whom thou lovest. This reminds one of the sentiments contained in the Persian poet Attar's lines. —

"No rank vain glory for me; I would sooner have pain of Love — its longings — its yearnings; — for Love's pain is man's sole *birth-right* — Angels feel it not though they may feel Love.

Insipid would be the possession of both the Worlds if thy heart is void of Love's ecstacy of pain — its yearnings — its hopes.

Let the infidel delight in his infidelity and the believer in his faith — an atom of Love's anguish would disengage Attar's heart of both — Then grant me O thou who art my pain's relief the pain of thy Love which alone is my Life".

According to the Sufi Doctrine the component units of this great integer the Universe, are but the bubbles that bubble out of one ocean of Love. In its bubble state, the individual bubble has its activities and movements in proportion to its limited capacity. But *while* it is merged in the endless ocean it is the ocean that acts, with its unlimited powers and activities, and not the bubble. We shall relate now one or two instances out of the many of the super-natural powers assigned to this Saint.

Once an old acquaintance who knew him in his former days of kingly power saw him on the banks of the Tigris sewing his patched garment. He taxed him for what he had left in exchange for a poor derwish's life. The saint threw his needle into the water below and a thousand fishes came out, each with a gold needle in its tiny mouth. The saint demanded his own and a tiny fish came out with his needle and raising its head placed it (the needle) at his feet.

The true derwish never asks any favours of others for himself, for he is resigned to the will of his Lord. It so happened that Ibn Adham had to remain without food for seven successive days. He was more thankful to his Lord, for he was nearer Him, for "the Lord loveth the Patient". On the seventh day pressed down by hunger he said "I ask of Thy Mercy to give me food". Presently a youth appeared before him and invited him to dinner. The saint was led to a spacious mansion richly furnished. When the host gazed at him attentively he recognised him and exclaimed "Of a sure thou art Ibne Adham my master. I am thy slave whom thou didst purchase when thou wast king of Balkh, and all this is of thy bestowal and legally thine". The saint granted the slave his freedom and all that legally belonged to him (Ibne Adham) and left the place saying "I will never ask my Lord again for myself".

One of the most pathetic stories related about this saint is the meeting between the father and the son, between the husband and his wife, after a lapse of many years. Ibne Adham's only son was a child when his father left his family amidst such romantic circumstances as we have described. When the Prince grew up he yearned to meet his father. With his Queen-mother and four thousand attendants the Prince set out for the pilgrimage of Hajj, as he knew that his father was at Mecca at that time. When he arrived there he was informed that his father went daily to the forest to cut wood. The Prince next day took the way to the forest and saw the Saint carrying a pack of wood on his back to sell it in the bazaar. The Prince's heart was touched. His father seemed also to recognise him. Next day one of the saint's disciples brought the Prince with his mother in the presence of his father. Paternal love surged in his heart and he embraced his son warmly and seated him on his lap. He questioned him as to his creed, whether he knew the Koran and had any share of learning. The Prince answering in the affirmative his father's heart was filled with joy. Meanwhile the people gathered to see this strange interview and said unto one another "Now will he leave us and his noble work for the people". The saint suddenly exclaimed "O Lord protect us", and the Prince lay dead in his arms. The people exclaimed "What has befallen thee Ibne Adham". The saint replied "Divine Inspiration came unto me and whispered in my heart 'wouldst thou now claim a selfless love for us'; and I prayed 'Oh Lord if my love for Thee is not selfless then part one of us from the other'. The arrow hit the mark against my son".

Every noble sentiment born of Divine Love, though small in its extents and activities at its birth, finding a congenial place in the human mind, and fed by the sweet waters of love, rises and swells into larger and still larger proportions, irrigating and fertilizing many a barren thought on its onward march, till it joins the ocean from which it derived its original waters, and assumes the ocean's activities and movements. This is illustrated in the holy Koran where the Lord says of Ibrahim the Prophet of God — "And so did we show Abraham the domain of the Heavens and of the Earth that he might be one of those who are stablished in knowledge". "And when the night overshadowed him he beheld a star. "This" said he "is my Lord": but when it set he said "I love not those that set". "And when he beheld the moon uprising "This" said he "is my Lord", but when it set he said "Surely if my Lord guide me not I shall be of those who go astray".

"And when he beheld the sun uprise he said" "This is my Lord this is greatest" but when it set he said "Oh my people I share not with you the guilt of joining Gods with God". "I verily turn my face to Him who hath created the Heavens and the Earth turning aside (from everything else) and I am not one of those who take Partners with the Lord".

The prophet's thought rests a while on the twinkling beauty of the gem-like star but he feels conscious of its setting. Then the moon, the Queen of night, with her soft beauty appeals to his imagination. But she too obeys the same law. Then his imagination goes forward and views the sun with its eye-piercing light and brilliant rays. But his reason concludes that all these powerful agencies are subservient to the fixed laws set for them by their Divine Master whose must be the Supreme Beauty, the Supreme Power, the Supreme Wisdom, and who suffers no decline of any sort, and the prophet exclaims "Verily I turn my face towards Him turning aside from everything else. Henceforth Divine Love rises superior to every obstacle in his way, he recks not every threat, every insult, and ignominy, even the torture of burning alive in fire; it rises above the supreme parental love that rises in his bosom and he is resigned to His will when ordered tc sacrifice his son.

In conclusion we give below some of the words assigned to this Saint.

1. Markst thou the man who knoweth his Lord; his mind is always contemplating and taking lessons; and his tongue uttereth those lessons in praise of his Creator's goodness; his acts are subservient to the Divine will; and his mental eye is always engaged in discovering the beauties of his Creator's Art in what His hands have wrought.

2. The traveller on this path has three curtains before his eye; when he removes them he sees the treasure he is in search of. Were he offered the kingdom of both the worlds he should not rest contented, for whosoever is satisfied with the created forsaking his Creator is selfish and the selfish in the

end is disappointed. Secondly, were the kingdom of both the worlds snatched away from him he should not grieve for the loss, for this shows narrowness of mind; — and the narrow-minded shall be punished; thirdly, he should not allow any flattery or bestowal to seduce him for it shows a lack of loftiness of spirit to be thus tempted away from one's purpose, and the low spirited is confined in a narrow sphere out of which he cannot come".

3. "Tie what thou openest and untie what thou tiest, i.e., tie thy tongue and untie thy purse strings."

4. (To one who had wronged his soul and asked the way to be righteous).

"When thou thinkest of doing wrong, do it after thou hast done these six things. — Partake not of thy daily bread for it is of His bounty — Take thee out of His protection and His kingdom and do it where He seeeth thee not — for it is shame adding unto shame to do it under His very eyes while thou eatest of His bounty and livest under His kingdom. Turn away the Angel of Death when he cometh to take thy life away — and the two Angels "*Munkar*" and "*Nakir*" when they come to question thy spirit after thy passing away from this life "who is thy Lord". — Refuse thou to take the path to Hell when they lead the righteous to Heaven and the wrongdoer to Hell. If thou canst not do these six things then prepare thee against Death before it overtakes thee; know thy Lord before the question is put to thy spirit "Who is thy Lord"; and be of the righteous so that the angels may lead thee to Heaven."

5. I have four chargers to ride upon — I ride on gratefulness to meet His bounty; on sincerity when going forth to do any righteous deed; on patience to battle with a hardship; on repentance to meet His forgiveness".

CONCLUSION.

The famous poet of Shiraz in one of his odes says "Last night I saw the Angels knocking at the door of the wine-house; — they kneaded Adam's clay with wine".

The wine house surely is in its full swing.

Every new comer has his destined cups given to him in the ever circulating round by the hands of the Divine Cupbearer. But the cups are however mixed with their wine-dregs. It is left to the drinker's choice not to allow the fumes to raise false phantasies before his eyes preventing him to see the Cup-bearer's Divine Beauty. Every cup should reveal to him a new charm, a new beauty in the cup bearer hidden before; till when his spirit is fully intoxicated with these Divine Love Cups, losing his "self" in the unconsciousness that should follow, nothing should remain before his mental eye but the Supreme-Beauty of the Creator. Then he should have acquitted himself of the Divine "Trust offered to the Heavens and the Earth and the mountains but the burden of which they were not equal to bear" but which as Hafiz says "fell to the lot of a poor madcap in love like himself".

Saints of Islam.

CHAPTER III.

ST. JUNAID OF BAGDAD AND HIS TIME.

Junaid was born in the year 232 A.H. at Bagdad where his father and uncle lived. His uncle was the most pious man of his time and Junaid being his favourite was brought up under his special care. He showed exceptional abilities from his childhood. When he was seven years old his uncle took him to Mecca with him in the season of Hajj. It is said that in the Sacred Musjid or Harem of Mecca where three hundred great divines of the time had gathered to meet his uncle and to discuss religious matters with him, the discussion turning upon what is "gratitude", the child's opinion was asked about it. He replied "Gratitude is appreciating the gift of the giver and not abusing it but making the best use of it". Every one admired this answer from a boy of seven years. When Junaid grew up he set up a business of glassware but his spare hours he spent in thinking and acquiring knowledge, and his nights in prayers and silent contemplation. When he had spent about thirty years in this way the people began to know of his great abilities and the goodness of his character. It is said that some of his enemies poisoned the ears of the Khalif of the time against him and he thought of finding a plausible excuse to disgrace him. The Khalif had a beautiful slave-girl who was his great favourite and who had no equal to her in point of beauty in his harem. He ordered her to put on her best dress and deck herself with the royal jewels and to go before Junaid and say to him after suddenly removing the veil from her face and disclosing her beauty before his ravished eyes "Sire my heart is turned cold to the affairs of this world. Henceforward I long to remain at thy feet, taking instruction from thy holy lips, and serve thee as the meanest of thy servants. He also instructed a confident servant to follow the girl secretly and to inform him of what happened. The girl did as she was bid to do. Junaid lifted up his head from the silent thoughts in which he was immersed and looked at her beautiful face and heaved a heavy sigh. The girl was, it seems, so affected, that she gave up her ghost and fell dead at his feet. The servant went and told what had occured, to the Khalif. He now repented of the hasty step he took in the matter but he saw that he could not blame Junaid in the matter and that he should not have tried to delude thus an innocent person into a trap. This incident however, came to the knowledge of the people and it raised Junaid's name and reputation amongst them. He now began to preach to the people. The purity of his thoughts added to his great mental abilities and the goodness of his character contributed to work a great change in the sentiments of the people. He was a very effective speaker and is said to have impressed his hearers a good deal. But before proceeding further we should survey briefly the preceding century and a half of the Mahomedan Hejira as far as it bears to our present subject. We should also give in a few concise words the spirit of Sufi Philosophy of Islam of which Junaid was one of the greatest exponents. The Ummayid dynasty had fallen. It was supplanted by the Abbaside Khalifs (or Caliphs as expressed by the Europeans) popularly known as the Khalifs of Bagdad. During the reign of the second ruler of this dynasty Al-Mansur, the foundation of the world-renowned city of Bagdad was laid. There is an interesting story regarding the building of this great city. The first sovereign of this Abbaside dynasty had built a palace for himself outside the town of Kufa the Capital of the Ummayaiids, and a new town had sprung up around it. During the disturbances that followed after him, the second Khalif thinking his life unsafe in that town, ordered his engineers to make every preparation for the purpose of building a great city, and he himself with his two Amirs went to search for a proper site for this purpose. He came near the place where the present city of Bagdad is situated and seeing a Christian monastery and a monk engaged in devotion therein he told his Amir to enter the monastery and question the monk about the suitability of the site for building a great city. The monk after giving a favourable report of the site asked the name of the Khalif. He was told that it was Mansur, whereupon he answered "This Khalif won't be able to build a city here for I have found in an old book left by my predecessors here, that a king of the name of Miklas will build here a great city which will be famous throughout the world. The Amir returned and told the Khalif what the monk had said. Hearing it the Khalif alighted from his horse and laying his head on the bare ground thanked his Lord. The Amir was surprised and questioned him why he had done so, whereupon he said "When I was quite a boy we were in very straightened circumstances as the Umayiid Khalif then in in power and his adherents were very hard upon us looking upon us as rivals to the throne. My young companions and myself used to make small picnic parties and our rule was that each of us should pay the expense of the party by turn. I could not find anything with me to defray its expense when my turn came, and looking about here and there, I found my nurse's threads of which she used to weave strings lying about. I pocketed them and sold them in the bazaar and paid my share of the picnic expense. When my nurse missed the threads she thought that I must be the young rogue that had stolen them and she questioned me and found out where her threads had gone. She nick-named me Miklas (thief) and used to call me by that name. No one knew the secret except the nurse and myself. The monk has augured well". The Khalif instantly gave his engineers orders to build the city.

As we have already alluded to before, the simplicity and purity of life and the selfless desire for truth and self-sacrifice for it, which had characterised the companions of the Prophet and the first votaries of Islam and which had already begun to ebb during the time of the Ummayiid Khalifs continued in its ebb even after these Khalifs, and during the spring time of the Bagdad Khalifs had completely changed into a luxury of living and indulgence in the pleasures of life which ultimately snapped the foundation of the great Khalifat (rule of the Khalifs) of Bagdad, and gave the reins of government into the hands of Turkish slaves, owned by these Khalifs. Ultimately they usurped the throne and became the rulers. The greatest Khalif of the Abbaside dynasty was Harun Ar Rashid. Though wilful and proud, he had a strong character and unbending will. In the internal administration of the state, and in extending the Mahomedan sway his hand was strong and descended with a force which was quite necessary in those stirring times to maintain a growing empire.

Harun Ar Rashid had a strong sense of duty and loved to get direct information regarding his subjects. He used sometimes therefore to put on the garb of a tradesman or derwish and mix with the people and enjoy their hospitality of an evening. The stories in the "Arabian Nights" regarding him have a nucleus of truth around them out of which such a nebulous globe of fiction has been spun out. He had a high appreciation of the true dervishes and whenener he grew tired of the worries of State-affairs he sought consolation in their company and took to his heart much plain spoken and homely advice uttered from their lips. One evening he went with his Vazir to see a well known pious derwish of his time, Fasil bin Ayaz, and sought admittance to his house. The saint was reading the Koran and had come to the verse "Deem they who earn evil unto them that We will deal with them as We deal with those who believe and do righteous deeds?". The Khalif said to his Vazir "If we need any advice, this verse is sufficient unto us". They then knocked at the door and in answer to the Saint's inquiry the Vazir said "It is the Commander of the Faithful who seeks admittance to thy house". "I have nothing to do with the Commander of the Faithful" was the reply; whereupon the Vazir reminded him that he was bound to obey the Khalif according to the words of God "Oh ye who believe obey God and obey the Apostle, and those among you invested with authority". They entered the room of the Saint. He put out the light that he might not be disturbed in his prayers and the hand of the Khalif happening to fall upon him, in the darkness, he remarked "What a well-formed hand is this! Would that the Khalif not besmear it with evil deeds and save it from the fire of God's anger". The Khalif was touched and asked for some words of sound advice whereupon he said "Thy ancestor was the Prophet's uncle and he asked of him to appoint him a ruler over an Arab clan. The Prophet replied "Remember and control thyself" meaning thereby self control and discipline should precede and is far superior to ruling over others, for without self-discipline many a time sovereignty results in repentance on the day of Judgment. Harun asked for more and the saint replied "Before thee was a good Khalif Umar Ibne Abdul Aziz who when he came in power asked the good counsel of a pious man and he said "If thou desirest to acquit thyself worthy of this office, regard the old amongst thy subjects as thou wouldst regard thy own father and the young as thou wouldst thy brother and the child as thy own child and regard the woman amongst them as thou wouldst thy mother and sister and deal with them accordingly; for thy kingdom is like unto thy own household and thy subjects its members; then be a support unto them in their helplessness as thou wouldst like to be unto thy father in his old age; be kind and lenient unto them as thou wouldst unto thy brother, and instruct and nourish them as thou instructeth and nourisheth thy children.

"God has appointed a good house which He hath named Heaven, and a bad one which he hath named Hell. He hath made thee in thy time warder of these two houses as regards thy subjects. For it depends to a great degree upon how thou dealest with thy subjects that they take virtue's path which leads to Heaven or the wrong path to Hell; for thy lax administration will encourage them to lawlessness and vice and thy proper administration will give them opportunities to take the better path. If an old woman amongst thy subjects to-day remains without food for a single day, through the neglect of thy duty towards them, thou shalt have to answer for it tomorrow before thy Lord on the day of Judgment". It is said the Khalif was so touched with these words that he left the pious man's house with tears in his eyes. Harun's son Mamun who succeeded him maintained the traditions of his father, and his able rule was conspicuous for Mahomedan victories over the Roman empire and the extension of Mahomedan sway. But the chief thing of interest to us is that his conquests brought the Greek classics and great works of the Greek mind within the reach of Muslim thinkers. Aristotle and other great works were translated into Arabic and the people's mind always inclined to religious philosophy turned to it more than ever.

The instruction which one derives directly from a really great and ingenious mind who has been gifted by nature with supernatural powers which enable him to read its book of hidden secrets and derive lessons from it which others cannot, is of a far superior kind to that which the after-generation derives from words and works which the instructor leaves after him as a legacy for mankind in general. To know personally a great and true instructor, to keep company with him, to be allied closely with him in the ties of friendship and love, to know his character in private and in public, to be a partner in his joys and sufferings, to feel in some degree what he feels, to imbibe the true spirit of his thoughts, to know every lane and avenue, whether spiritual or otherwise which has led to these thoughts, is a far superior kind of instruction to that derived by after-generation from the words assigned to him, or any work left by him, whether divinely given to him and brought into existence through his spiritual agency, or the mere product of his own intellect. It is specially so in the case of religious instruction, where the ignorant mind is apt to take only a literal view and cannot feel the abstract idea; or when he looks only to the outward form and features of religion, however graceful and beautiful, but cannot feel the inward spirit and the noble feelings that are even depicted in the mirror of the external form and which even an untutored mind endowed with an artistic eye sometimes does not fail to discern.

Among every nation, it is the interest of the class of priests who have to depend for their means of sustenance on what they receive from the people for their preaching to them, or who have no worthier desire than to gain cheap notoriety among the masses, to endeavour to keep them confined to the mere letter of religion, and its outward form and ceremonies, which often inclines the people to be narrow-minded and bigoted and breeds an intolerance in them of a broad and unconfined view of religion. The purity and expanse of religious thought which had characterised the first four Khalifs after the Prophet, and the generality of Mahomedans in their time, had gradually given way to a great degree to intolerance of free thoughts and a preponderance of the priestly class we have above alluded to. In direct contrast in their views and sentiments to this class, another school of thinkers had risen who called themselves Sufis and who taught religion in its noblest aspect, and as Junaid was one of its best exponents it will be interesting to give here in a few words the spirit of the Sufi Philosophy of Islam.

THE WHOLE UNIVERSE A REFLECTION OF DIVINE LIGHT; THE REFLECTION, NOT THE REALITY; THE SHADOW NOT THE SUBSTANCE.

Their ideas about the Deity although approaching in some ways to pantheism were not really pantheistic for they did not subscribe to the belief that the whole Universe is God Himself but that it is only a reflection of Divine Light, the shadow, but not the real substance, or in other words it is the Divine attributes working and moving and appearing in innumerable different lights and colours. Creation is only the mirror in which a million different movements of one, all-comprising Divine attribute of "Love" in its multifarious phases are seen. The perfect human being is the best in creation, for, possessing the full scope of attaining pure and selfless Love, he has attained it after passing through many a trial and barrier set before him and the attainment ot his object.

Pleasure and pain, joy and sorrow, pride and humility, in fact every opposite feeling owes its birth and existence to the one all-encompassing feeling of "Love." But Love in its perfect form is Divine Love shorn of all "self" looking to the loved one alone.

KNOWLEDGE AND SELF INSTRUCTION.

Just as in an ordinary love-affair between a man and a woman, the love which originates in a lover by his taking a fancy to, and being drawn away and attracted by some peculiar and remarkable traits in the character of the loved one, an inward beauty rather than an outward charm in her, that Love rests on a more solid foundation than that which owes its birth to the mere attraction of outward beauty; so the flame of Divine Love can only be fully kindled when the inward and unclouded vision, penetrating through the outward garb of nature, finds out the Divine spirit that is working underneath and which is the life and essence of all creation. According to the Sufi derwishes the traveller on this path of Divine Love should take as his text "I (the Lord) was a hidden treasure and loved to be sought out" which implies that the ultimate object of the Creator in the evolution of creation was that He should be known as He is; and this knowledge can only be attained through the avenue of pure and selfless love.

TRUE PIETY.

Taking these principles as his basis the Sufi derwish builds his moral edifice upon it. Piety according to him has two sides external and internal; the external lies in keeping oneself confined to the limits set down by the moral law of religion; the internal in the sincerity and purity of thought which should precede action. Although admitting that specified prayers and other acts of piety contribute to some degree in elevating one's character, he thinks that the true moral elevation lies in making love one's Musjid and turning to the *Kibla* of Divine will, in offering the sacred *Nimaz* of self-effacement. The true fast according to him is the moral fast of abstaining from everything forbidden by the sacred law of Love; and the true *Zakat*, the *Zakat* of self-sacrifice and spending one's mental and physical powers for the good of one's fellow-creatures for the mere love of his Lord.

DEALINGS WITH OUR FELLOW-BROTHERS.

"Faith is Good-Will" said the Prophet and he repeated his words thrice to give force to them. Faith must have its edifice on the firm basis of good-will towards all and a clear conscience with the Lord and His creatures. But good-will attains perfection when the spirit of self-sacrifice, of placing other people's good before one's own, is exercised and put into practice.

KINDLING OF LOVE'S DIVINE FLAME.

Human society is based on Love and whatever position one enjoys in the social scale he gets ample opportunities to exercise his faculty of Love. But that feeling which is meanly exercised to gain a selfish end, or for the indulgence of a short-lived pleasure, is not the pure substance but a mixture which requires the fire of trial to purify it of its dross. Unlike any other commodity Love cannot be made a bargain of; for if it be given in return for any selfish object in view, it vanisheth when that object is gained or when there is no hope of attaining that object. It should be kindled purely, for when purely kindled it is returned purely. It requires awakening but when it echoes its sound clearly through the human heart, without the voice of self mixed with it, it is sure of a pure and unmixed response. As a Persian poet says:

"A balm can only be applied where there is pain". "A difficult problem is soon solved when the pressing necessity of its solution arises". "Just as the waters always find a low ground for their flowing out, the sweet response of Love flows for him who is smitten down by it". "How sweet the appeasing of one's trying thirst, but thou canst not have this appeasing delight without first feeling thirsty". "The child when it crieth with hunger its mother gives it suck; and the cloud of mercy pours water on the parched land."

THE DEVELOPEMENT OF THE SENSES.

The machinery of the senses should be so put in action that every wheel respectively of each sense should work and turn out pure stuff of love, the spiritual engineer of Divine Love guarding it from its turning out waste-matter.

The sense of sight should be so engaged that every glance should endeavour to find out a new beauty in nature, every thought to trace out a new art in what her hands have wrought. The sense of hearing should be exercised to listen to the voice of nature all around. The gentle tunes of birds varying in a thousand varieties each sweet though different to the other, the sweet sound of the flowing waters, the gentle murmur of the winds, the love-exciting notes of the string instruments and above all the Divinely melodious human voice singing the sad tale of Love, all this listened with a contemplative mind adds to the warmth of the pure flame which has been kindled in one's heart and gives him the sweet and sad pleasure, the ecstacy of love which the Lover's heart yearneth for. As a Persian poet sings. —

"What pleasure can sweet viands give!
For me sweet kisses of love,
Though preceded by trial's hard things;

Sweet were the words of that charming cup-bearer
Drink deep of this Love-cup, and speak not of it to those who are ignorant of its hidden pleasure."

TRIAL IN THE DURBAR.

Junaid and his disciples gradually began to exercise such a vast influence over the sentiments of the people that they became a thorn in the side of the narrowminded and bigotted clergy of their time. One of them who had a great influence with the Khalif poisoned his ears against them saying "These persons' propaganda lies only in teaching people how to love. They love music and everything that is beautiful in nature and preach to people the liberal ideas of the free thinking heretics". The saint and some of his chief followers were arraigned on a charge of preaching heresy to the people and brought before the Khalif in the full Darbar. The culprits were seated in a line and the executioner was ordered to do his deadly work. As he advanced towards one of them, another, Nuri by name, arose instantly and took the place of the intended victim. The Khalif was surprised at the man's eagerness to serve his brother derwish and save his life, even though it be for a few moments more, and he said to him "Thou but thinkest lightly of thy life to sell it so cheaply". He replied "It is the rule with us to prefer our fellow-brother's welfare to our own and afford him the enjoyment of whatever is dear and valuable to us. Think not that I regard my life lightly. I consider it as the most precious gift to me from Heaven, for every moment of it is precious to me, as I may use it to a good purpose and so stand in the service of the Lord that I may gain thereby His Eternal Nearness, and the ecstacy of seeing His Supreme Beauty". The Khalif was touched with these words and stopped the executioner from doing his work and referred the matter to the grand Cazi to be decided upon after a due inquiry. In those days of summary justice when it did not require any big briefs to be prepared, and a lengthy and costly process to be undergone, before the case came to be finally decided upon by the "learned Judge", the Cazi in the simple old fashion of our ancestors took up the case immediately in the presence of the Khalif. As a shrewd lawyer, for lawyers were shrewd in those days too, he thought to cross-examine one of the defendants whom he thought quite ignorant in matters theological. So he began. "If the true believer has twenty *dinars* in his possession, how much out of this is he bound to give in charity by the set rules of his faith"? The derwish answered "Twenty dinars and a half". The Cazi went on in triumph "Who ever didst such a sort of foolish thing"? "A far better man than thee, Cazi" said the derwish. "The first Khalif of the Faithful Abu Bikar had forty thousand dinars with him in the time when Islam was in its infancy and struggling for its very existence. He spared not a single coin out of it but spent it all in the way of the Lord, for he loved Him with a sincere love. An obedience to the rules set by our religion, no doubt requires a fraction of the amount one has, to be paid in charity, but true love requires that nothing should be spared to gain love in return."

"Thou speakest wisely" said the Cazi "but why should one give half a dinar more than he has?" "As a fine" said the derwish "for hesitating to spend where sincere love dictated it to be so spent; for true love dispels any idea of "self" in the lover". The Cazi baffled by the derwish's answer turned towards another and began to question him about the minor points of ecclesiastical law. The derwish after answering all his questions correctly, for the majority of these derwishes used to study religion in all its branches, said in the end "Cazi thou lookest only to the letter of religion, forsaking its spirit. Thou hadst better ask us what is the end and aim of all these laws set by religion. Knowest thou not O Cazi! that there are creatures of God upon this earth whose faith is Love. They live in His love and breathe His love-breaths. Their very heart-life is His love. They see with His eyes and hear with His ears and feel the divine feeling".

The Cazi said "Oh Khalif of the Muslims, if the accused are heretics then I decide that no true believer is left on our earth".

We give below an illustrative story taken from an Oriental work to show that when love the Sultan passion is recognised and given allegiance to, it underfetters all other passions and directing them into their proper channels gives them their full scope in the performance of the office assigned to them.

There was a king of old, who as was the custom of the Oriental kings in those times, changing his royal garb of an evening and putting on that of the common people, used to walk in the slums of the city to know personally the state of his subjects. One evening while taking such a walk he met with four persons who he thought were bent on doing a big job that night. He joined them saying "I am a bird of the same feather with you". Finding him a boon companion they soon became friendly with him. He inquired of each, of the particular art he knew whereupon one of them said "I understand the speech of the lower animals". His other companion said "I am gifted with such a sense of smell that I can find out with its aid where the treasure is hidden." The third said "I know the art of opening a lock however intricate it be". The fourth said "I am gifted with a power better than that which any of my other companions possesses, for if I happen to see once a person's face even in darkness, I can recognise him ever afterwards, though he be hid amongst a thousand people". They all inquired of the new friend what art he possessed whereupon he said "I possess this extraordinary power that if I chance to see a person sentenced to be hanged and if I nod my head at him he is at once set at liberty." "This is mighty good", they said, "and this should make us bold to-night to commit burglary on the king's treasury". They all set out together. In the midst of their way they met with a dog who barked at them. Their new friend asked of the one who knew the speech of the lower animals, "what does this dog say"? "It says", said he, "there is a king amongst you but refuses to say any further". When they came to the treasury, its locked door was opened by the companion who knew the art of opening intricate locks and they entered it and the treasure was soon searched out where it lay hidden, by the person who possessed the extraordinary sense of smell amongst them. After their work was over they separated and the king came to his palace. The next day it was given out that the king's treasure had been stolen during the night. After trying his officers' skill in tracing out the burglars, and finding them wanting in it, for there were no such clever detectives in those days as we have, though the thieves we believe did not yield to ours in point of their thieving intellect, the king gave the clue to his officers of the burglars' whereabouts. The burglars were tried in the Cazi's *kutcheri* and were sentenced to be hanged; but the king had given orders not to execute the punishment upon them without his order. When the burglars saw they would soon be hanged, the one amongst them possessed of acute distinguising powers said "I suspect the stranger who joined us in the burglary was the king himself for our companion interpreted the dog's bark as meaning 'there is a king amongst you'. Were I to see him I would soon recognise him though he be in his royal garb and state." They asked therefore of the warder to get permission of the king to allow them to come in his presence as they wanted to tell him something. They were ushered into the king's presence and the person blest with extraordinary distinguishing powers said to him "each of us has shown his art to thee. Now we ask of thy blessed head this favour to nod at us a little and free us from the gallows for truly enough it possesseth the power of saving persons from the gallows".

The king's head nodded politely at them and set them at their liberty. The king gave each of them an office congenial to his abilities. Thus love the Sultan-passion when recognised and given allegiance to unfetters the thieves of passions and gives them honest and congenial work to do.

We give below some of the sentiments of the saint and his followers comparing them with similar sentiments by other Oriental thinkers.

LOVE.

1. Junaid. —

Love is a sacred trust, a heavenly gift,

placed in the human heart, to be spent only for receiving pure love in return. For, unlike other things, it cannot be made a bargain of. If it be bartered for the gratification of a selfish desire, or for the indulgence of a short-lived pleasure, when such desire or pleasure is satisfied the sacred trust is taken away for its abuse and is seldom replaced again. Love is perfect between two persons when one can say to the other "Thou art me and "vice versa;" an entire disappearance of the Lover's individuality. Compare this sentiment with the similar one in the Koran "We offered this trust (of pure Love) to the skies and the earth and the mountains but they refused to bear up the burden and were afraid of the heavy charge but man took it up; verily he was oppressive in this to himself and ignorant (of the responsibility involved in it).

2. Shibli. —

The heart wherein Thy Love dwelleth does not require any other lamp, for Thy love-light removeth its darkness; when on that day of reward and retribution people put forth what they did to get their expected meed, our proof shall lie in the love we bore Thee where all our hopes were centred.

3. Junaid. —

If all thy merits cannot win His nearness thy merits are in truth demerits. Compare the similar sentiment in Sadi.

"Let Philosophers claim sense as the best gift of nature but those who know Thee say that the intoxication of Thy Love is far sweeter."

Compare also Saint Rabia's prayer. —

"O Thou who knoweth the heart's secrets grant thou the pleasures of this world to him who desireth; and of the next to him who striveth for them. Only grant Thyself unto me for Thou art all in all unto me."

MAGNANIMITY.

4. Junaid.

Magnanimity consists in not laying thy burden upon another and that what thou hast thou spendest in another's cause.

Compare Sadi.

"True nobility lies in spending what thou hast for another's cause and true honour in laying thy face in humble adoration before thy Lord."

5. Ibne Ata. —

True piety has two sides, the external and the internal; the external lies in keeping oneself confined to the limits set down by the moral law of religion, the internal in the sincerity and purity of thought which precedes thy action.

Compare the Koran.

"There is no piety in turning your faces towards the East or the West, but he is pious who believeth in God and the Last Day and the Angels and the Scriptures and the Prophets; who for the Love of God disburseth his wealth to his kindred and to the orphans and the needy and the way-farer, and to those who ask for charity and for freeing the necks fettered in slavery; who observeth prayer and payeth the purifying alms and who is one of those who are faithful to their engagements when they have engaged in them, and patient under ills and hardships and in time of trouble: these are true in their faith, and these are the truly pious."

6. Shibli. —

The pure in heart are nourished in the lap of His Love and fed with the milk of His kindness like the child who is fed and nourished by its loving parent.

7. Sirri Sikti. (Junaid's uncle and Instuctor). The pure in heart like earth receiveth every evil and giveth in return its fruitful product.

THE PURE IN HEART WHO KNOWETH HIS LORD.

8. Shibli. —

The life-time of the pure in heart who knoweth his Lord may be likened unto the aspect of nature in spring time wherein the water-cloud smileth and the thunderbolt consumeth, the thunder soundeth and the breeze bloweth, sweet flower of every kind blossometh and the bird intoxicated with the beauty of the time poureth forth its soul; so the righteous man's eyes shed tears while his lips smile; his heart burns and is consumed with the fire of Love lit in it, while he like a fond bird in love with the flowers and intoxicated with the beauty, utters the praises of his Lord.

9. Sirri Sikti- —

The pure in heart who knoweth his Lord is like the sun which sheddeth its lusture for all, irrespective of any person or place, and like the earth which beareth the weight of the high and the low, even like unto water which possesseth the life-giving property and like the lamp from which other lights are kindled.

GRATITUDE.

10. Junaid.

Gratitude is appreciating the gift of the giver and not abusing it but making the best use of it.

11. Gratitude is looking to the giver and not to the gift.

MAGNANIMITY.

12. Junaid. —

Magnanimity lies in forgetting any obligation thou hast done to others and not mentioning it as "I have done this for you" nor even ascribing it to thyself.

13. Abu Hafs.

Magnanimity lies in giving justice to others and not standing on receiving justice from others.

14. THE FEAR OF THE LORD.

The fear of the Lord is the Lamp by which thou canst distinguish the good and the evil that is contained in thee.

INTERPRETING FEELINGS.

15. Sirri Sikti. —

Thy manners and words interpret thy feelings and thy face is the mirror wherein thy heart is reflected.

THREE KINDS OF CHARACTER.

16. Siri Sikti.

Three kinds of character the men possess
One like the mountain firm and obdurate
Nothing can remove him from his place
The other like the tall firm rooted tree
Moved now and then by storms and winds
The last is like the feather, borne by the
wind where'er it turneth.

GOOD TEMPER.

17. Sirri Sikti. —

Good temper lies in not offending another's feelings and forbearing with him if thou receivest injury from him, seeking not any retaliation.

THE STORIES ABOUT THE RIGHTEOUS.

18. Junaid. —

The stories related about the righteous are like the hosts of angels from Heaven, to guard and guide thee on thy way.

Compare Jami (Persian poet).

"When thou hast set up the idols of good intentions within thy mind breathe unto them the preserved breaths of the righteous and they will rise up into moving actions and realities. If evil passions create an earthquake in thy heart charm them into silence by the magic words of the truly righteous."

www.ingramcontent.com/pod-product-compliance
Lightning Source LLC
Chambersburg PA
CBHW062143160726
48282CB00027B/930

* 9 7 8 9 3 6 6 0 8 4 3 2 9 *